£8-95

# Lace Flowers
## and how to make them

# Lace Flowers
## and how to make them

### by Joyce R. Willmot

RUTH BEAN Carlton Bedford

Published by Ruth Bean, Victoria Farmhouse, Carlton, Bedford MK43 7LP, England.

ISBN 0 903585 23 5

Design, James Skelton
Photography, Photographic Department, Cambridge University Library
Cover photograph, Nigel Bean
Printed in Great Britain by Jolly & Barber Ltd, Rugby.

**Plates with captions**

# Contents

Figure 1
Victorian wax flower arrangement reproduced in lace by the author. An early effort.

# Introduction

To the dismay of my teacher I never wanted to do 'yardage lace' and as soon as I was able to master the basic techniques I tried to find ways of adapting those techniques to new ideas. I started making lace pictures, using embroidery transfers as patterns or preparing my own prickings from existing prints, as well as by using collage methods.

But one day back in the early seventies I came across a long-forgotten Victorian glass dome in a cupboard. It was a small dome with white wax flowers, probably from a wedding cake. This gave me the idea that I could make a similar type of arrangement—in lace. The flowers were imaginary ones so I copied their shapes and prepared prickings. My teacher was rather doubtful about my collection of loose petals, but my class friends were intrigued by the end result (Fig 1). This encouraged me to continue and gave me the idea to copy real flowers. The first effort was a snowdrop followed by a selection of wild flowers for which I have a great love. I also found great pleasure in exploring the use of colour. To my delight I was asked to hold a special workshop on lace flowers, which was soon followed by many more both in this country and abroad.

The method combines traditional lace techniques with the cheerful use of colour to create a three dimensional likeness to familiar flowers, and this pleased many lace-makers. The materials themselves are not required in large quantities, even the thread. Moreover, despite popular belief, the lace flowers require no starching. My students have often suggested that I write a book about it, and here it is at last! In preparing the patterns for the petals and leaves I have tried to follow each flower and its colouring as closely as possible. I have also varied the use of stitches to give certain flowers a lighter appearance. These techniques lend themselves very well to improvisation and readers can adapt them to their particular ideas and create variations of their own.

I would like to thank Mrs Joan Buckle for encouraging me during my early days of making lace flowers to take on workshops, which have given me so much pleasure. I am indebted to both Mrs Buckle and Mrs Dorothy Cox for urging me to write a book on making flowers. I would like to thank Ruth and Nigel Bean for the care they have taken with all aspects of the book and Mrs Maria Rutgers for her work on the diagrams. My gratitude goes to Mrs Pat Lord for her companionship in so many shared lace-making activities over the years. I wish to thank Mrs Pat Harris of Portland, Oregon, who has contributed so tirelessly to lace-making in her part of the world, for her friendship and encouragement.

Joyce R Willmot

# How to use the book

The book is in two parts. Part one sets out a detailed inventory of the materials, lace-making and assembly techniques needed to make any flower and leaf shown in the book. Two basic stitches with several variations are used to work all the petals and leaves. To this are added instructions for setting in, ways of working the edges, adding pairs, adding a gimp, tying off at the end and so on. These are explained in detail together with the appropriate diagrams. Two practice petals are given to demonstrate the stitches and their variations. A chapter on making leaves not worked in lace, as well as a note on display and on making one's own design are included.

Part two comprises the individual flowers, arranged roughly to follow the seasons; with the red-green-silver orchid spray completing the year. The text and illustrations for each flower is set out on facing pages as a self-contained unit. It gives the materials and quantities required, working instructions, specific points on assembly and display, prickings and working diagrams as necessary. A photograph of the finished display is given with each flower and a selection of displays in full colour appear in the centre of the book. The prickings are shown in actual size and the following symbols are used:

    **x** indicates the starting point
    • shows where to add pairs at the edges
    ∩ shows where to add pairs in the centre of a petal or leaf
    ↕ shows the line for hand-stitching

The botanical notes (p 70) are intended as an additional source of information.

# PART I MATERIALS AND TECHNIQUES

## MATERIALS

### Lace-making

Materials for the lace-making parts of the flowers are obtainable from specialist suppliers. A selected list is given on p 73.

    Pillow: a small pillow is sufficient (12 in or 30 cm wide)

    Bobbins: all types of bobbins are suitable (including other European ones)

    Card for prickings

    Pins: fine pins, 1 to $1\frac{1}{2}$ in (25 to 40 mm) long

    Thread: white DMC 30 Retors d'Alsace; Mettler 30 coloured cotton or any other coloured cotton thread of equivalent thickness in the colours suggested; Clark's Anchor embroidery thread (use only one of the six strands at a time); white or coloured sewing cotton (avoid the polyester type); Lamé thread—DMC 10 Fil d'Argent à broder; green cotton-covered fine wire ($\frac{1}{64}$ in or 0.46 mm) for use as a gimp in long leaves (Millinery wire or rose wire).

### The assembly of flowers

    Wire for the stems: stub wire or stem wire, $\frac{1}{32}$ in (0.9 mm) or thinner if available, as used by florists, also available from craft shops and garden centres.

    Stamens: specified for each flower. Craft and specialist shops sell a wide selection. For hand-made stamens use Clark's Anchor embroidery thread (all six strands).

    Floral tape to cover the stems: comes in a standard width of $\frac{1}{2}$ in (12 mm). This is a mat crepe paper impregnated to make it self-adhesive—avoid the shiny variety. It must be stored in a tightly sealed container to prevent it from drying out.

    Dry foam (Oasis or Floral pack) for the base of flower arrangements.

### Leaves not made from lace

    Wire for the stems: see above.

    Green contact paper with adhesive back: available from hardware shops and normally used to cover household goods.

    Silk leaves: available from florists and garden centres.

    Floral tape: same as described above under materials for the assembly of flowers, available from florists, garden centres or craft shops.

    Silk ribbon with adhesive back: available from specialist shops and normally used for making artificial flowers; suppliers listed on p 73.

    Natural leaves dried in preserving crystals: small preserving crystals can be obtained from suppliers listed on p 73 or from chemists.

# TECHNIQUES

## Lace-making techniques

Experienced lace-makers will be familiar with the methods set out for each flower. The following instructions are included for beginners and as a reminder of main points if required.

### Winding the bobbins

In order to save thread wind only one bobbin fully leaving a short length on the pairing bobbin.

### The stitches

*Cloth stitch (or whole stitch)*

Cloth stitch is worked with four threads. Place No 2 over No 3; then, keeping to the original numbering, put No 3 over No 1; No 4 over No 2; and No 1 over No 4. See Fig 2.

*Half-stitch*

This stitch is worked like the cloth stitch except that you omit the last movement. Work with four threads. Place No 2 over No 3; then, keeping to the original numbering, put No 3 over No 1 and No 4 over No 2. This completes the half-stitch. See Fig 3.

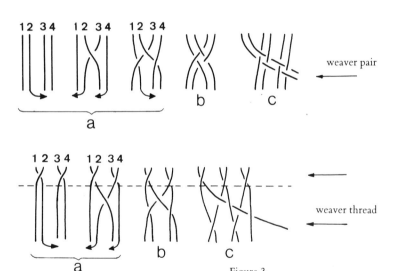

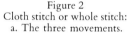
weaver pair

Figure 2
Cloth stitch or whole stitch:
a. The three movements.
b. The completed stitch.
c. Two completed stitches.

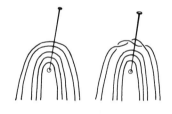
weaver thread

Figure 3
Half-stitch: a. The three movements.
b. The completed stitch.
c. Two completed stitches. Upper
arrow shows pairs hanging in readiness, twisted once.

Figure 4
Setting in and twisting the
outside pairs.

### Setting in (or setting up)

All flowers and leaves are started in the following way. Hang all the initial number of pairs open on the starting pin marked **x**, making sure that the pin slopes backwards (Fig 4); this will hold the threads in position. Twist the two outside pairs three times. You can start working either from the left or from the right. Using the twisted pair as a weaver, work across in either cloth stitch or half-stitch as indicated on the pattern. Figure 5 gives sample petals worked in either cloth stitch or half-stitch.

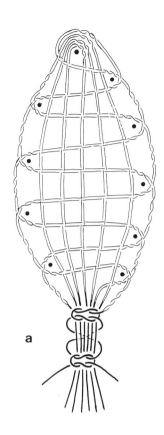

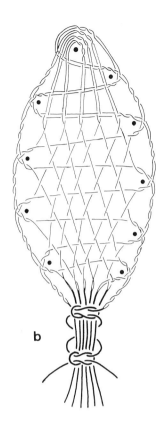

Figure 5
Sample petals:
a. Cloth stitch or whole stitch.
b. Half-stitch. Note that the
first 2 or 3 rows are worked
in cloth stitch.

a

b

## Working the edge

When making a *straight* edge, the last stitch is worked as follows. Twist the outside pair three times and the weaver twice. Then, regardless of the stitch in which the petal is being worked, work a cloth stitch, making sure that you put the pin between pair 2 and pair 3. Pair 2 will now be the weaver. Twist this weaver twice and work the row, leaving pair 1 unworked (this was the old weaver). Pair 1 will be worked on the return row (Fig 6). Continue in this way until the end of the pattern, unless the instructions state otherwise.

A straight edge is worked on all petals and leaves.

When a *serrated* edge is required as an alternative, for example on the rose leaf, work as follows. Work to the edge (that is, complete the row). Twist the weaver three times. Put the pin between the weaver and the first passive pair to hold the edge stitch in position. Work the return row with the same weaver (Fig 7).

## Adding pairs

To add an extra pair of bobbins, work as follows. Work the edge stitch, put in pin. Place the new pair under the weaver pair (Fig 8a), take up and bring round the pin to become pair 3 (Fig 8b & c). Now work the row and this will hold the added pair in position (Fig 8d).

Pairs added in the middle of a petal are hung open round a pin as passive pairs and worked in, as indicated on the pattern. A point to remember: leave the pin in until the pattern is completed.

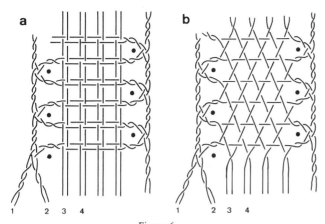

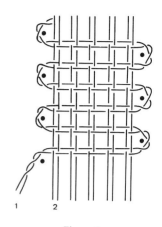

Figure 6
Working a straight edge: a. Cloth stitch with straight edges.
b. Half stitch with straight edges.

Figure 7
Cloth stitch with serrated edge.

## Ladder effect

Ladder effect is used to lighten the look of a cloth stitch area. Work as follows. Work to the centre of the petal or leaf and twist the weavers twice; this widens out the cloth stitch area. Continue to the edge of the row, return to the centre and increase the number of twists on the weavers to 4 or 5 as the pattern widens. Gradually decrease the number of twists as the pattern tails off to the end (see Plate 1: Nos 2, 4 & 5 or the Poppy p 50 etc).

## Lightening the texture

Another way to lighten the texture of a petal or leaf is to twist the weaver before working each passive pair. The number of twists can vary between one and three, and will increase the width of the mesh. The number of twists required will be given on each pattern (eg p 30 etc).

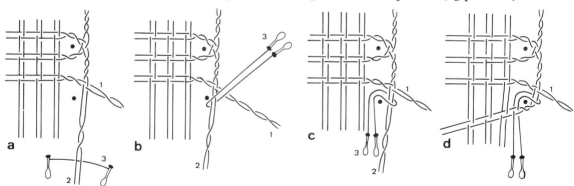

Figure 8
Adding a pair.

## Adding a gimp

A gimp is added to achieve a special design and to add texture, as for example in the Iris where full instructions are given (see p 42). I discovered this particular feature on an old Bedfordshire lace collar which I acquired some years ago in an antiques market. It was worked in the centre of leaves which formed the edge of the collar.

A fine green, cotton-covered, wire (millinery wire) can be worked as a gimp to provide stiffening for longer leaves such as those for snowdrops and daffodils. It is to be worked round the edges or down the centre in the same way as that done with thread gimp (see p 69).

Tying off at the end
Work the pattern to the last pin-hole and cover the last pin with a cloth stitch. Take the two outside pairs, leaving enough thread to make four knots. Cut off the threads from the two outside pairs and tie two knots on top. Holding all the bobbins bunched together, take the cut threads underneath the bobbins and cross them over. Bring the thread to the top and tie again. Cut off the remaining threads, leaving about $\frac{1}{2}$ in (12 mm) of thread (Fig 9a & b).

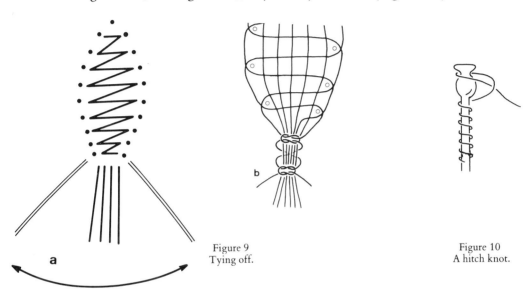

Figure 9
Tying off.

Figure 10
A hitch knot.

Leaves
I chose lace leaves for the canary bird rose, daisy, pansy and the fuchsia because their shapes lend themselves to lace stitches. Samples of lace leaves can be seen on Plate 1 and instructions are given with each of the above patterns. Elongated leaves can also be made in lace though a wire gimp needs to be used to give the necessary support. A special pattern is provided for this on p 69.

## Assembly techniques
Flowers
The flowers in this book are made up of a variety of components but the way in which they are put together is the same. The secret is to keep in mind the appearance of the living flower. The real thing is best but a coloured photograph or picture will be very helpful.

Before you start assembling the flowers you need to have in front of you the following: wires, tape, stamens, petals, leaves.

All stamens and petals are tied to the flower stem with a hitch knot, in the same way as the thread is secured to the head of the bobbin (Fig 10).

*Flowers with petals*

1. *Making the pad.* First place a small piece of $\frac{1}{2}$ in (12 mm) wide floral tape on the top end of a wire; fold over, pinch the tape close to the wire with your finger nail, pressing it tightly (Fig 11); roll between thumb and finger and cut off any surplus if it appears to be too thick. Covering the end of the wire provides a pad which will give the threads being tied on a grip and stop them from sliding. It will also mask the end of the wire which would otherwise be exposed when looking down into the flower.

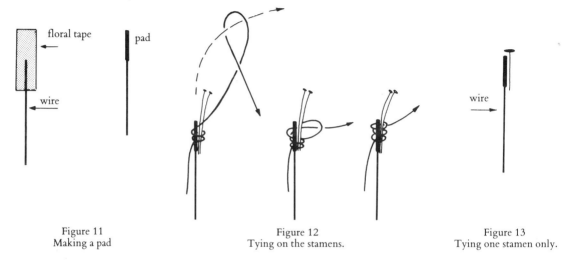

Figure 11
Making a pad

Figure 12
Tying on the stamens.

Figure 13
Tying one stamen only.

2. *Tying on the stamens.* Allow approximately $\frac{1}{2}$ yard (45 cm) of thread for tying on the stamens and petals, using the colour of the petals. Add the required number of stamens and tie them to the stem with a hitch knot (Fig 12).

When only one stamen is needed, it will rest right on top of the pad (Fig 13). When there are multiple stamens they will be spread evenly round the pad and tied with two to three hitch knots.

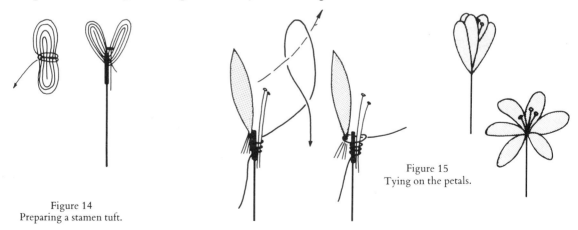

Figure 14
Preparing a stamen tuft.

Figure 15
Tying on the petals.

When a *stamen tuft* is required, work as follows. Wind the appropriate coloured cotton a number of times around two fingers. Remove and tie in the centre (Fig 14). Arrange the tuft round a single small stamen already tied to a wire stem. Tie tightly with a hitch knot. After the flower petals are secured in position, cut the loops of the cotton to form a little tuft.

3. *Tying on the petals.* Hold the base of the first petal against the base of the stamen or stamens at the point where the stamens are tied to the stem. With the thread used to tie the stamens tie the petal to the stem with a hitch knot. Repeat this for all the petals (Fig 15). When all petals are tied onto the wire stem, taper off any surplus threads to avoid unnecessary bulk on the stem.

4. *Taping the stem.* Hold the stem wire in one hand and the end of the tape in the other. Put the end of the tape on top of the tied threads right up to the base of the petals. Holding the stem and tape together, give the stem a few tight turns allowing the tape to cover all the stamen and petal ends. Press hard to secure it firmly.

Hold the tape at a downward angle, keeping it tightly tensioned (Fig 16). Rotate the stem between finger and thumb along the first finger. Remember—always rotate the stem along the tape, never try to wind the tape round the stem!

To finish off taping, cut tape at an angle and press in firmly.

Only after the stem has been taped arrange the petals. With the tip of your fingers gently curve the petals as necessary, always bearing in mind the appearance of the living flower.

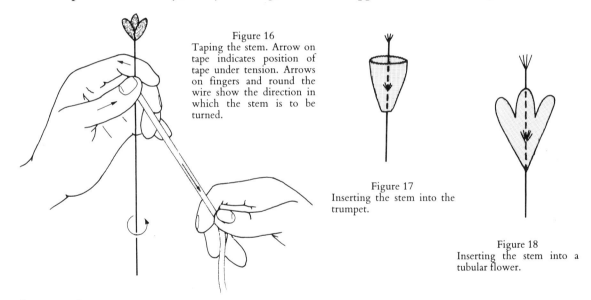

Figure 16
Taping the stem. Arrow on tape indicates position of tape under tension. Arrows on fingers and round the wire show the direction in which the stem is to be turned.

Figure 17
Inserting the stem into the trumpet.

Figure 18
Inserting the stem into a tubular flower.

*Flowers with a trumpet*
This section applies to daffodils and narcissi. Having stitched the trumpet as directed in the pattern and secured the required number of stamens to a stem, push the stem down into the trumpet as shown in Fig 17. When the stamen is in position tie the base of the trumpet with a hitch knot. To this you will add the outside petals, tying a petal at a time, until the the flower head is completed.

*Tubular flowers*
In the case of the freesia, the cyclamen and the winter jasmine, the flower head itself is a tube so proceed as directed above for flowers with a trumpet. However there will be no outside petals to add (Fig 18).

Leaves—making and assembling

Leaves are important to the final look of the arrangement so their making, taping and assembly need care. In this section basic guidelines are given on the preparation and assembly of the different kinds of leaves found in this book, while specific instructions are given with each flower.

As you can see on Plate 1, a variety of materials are available, but the choice for each flower has been made on the basis of the shape of the leaf. Smaller leaves lend themselves to lace-making stitches as mentioned above under Lace-making techniques. Longer lance-like leaves are made from floral tape or adhesive silk ribbon, though they can also be worked in lace (see p 69). Other materials and shapes are discussed below.

*Silk leaves*

Florists stock many types of silk leaves already mounted on a wire stem which can be cut to the required shape, as suggested in the patterns; for example the violet, cyclamen, orchid and primrose. The silk and lace combination works very well and will give your flower arrangement added texture.

*Leaves made with contact paper*

This material has an adhesive back. It is particularly suitable for leaves of the clematis and fuchsia.

For each leaf, cut out two identical pieces and peel off the protective layer. Take a length of wire and lay the wire between the two pieces, about $\frac{1}{4}$ in (6 mm) away from the tip of the leaf (Fig 19); press hard together. Trim to shape.

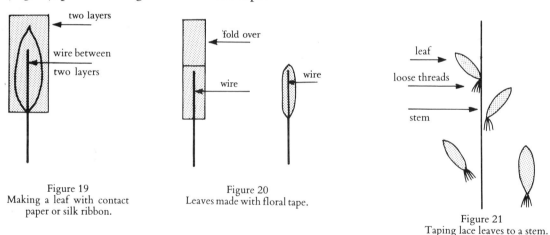

Figure 19
Making a leaf with contact paper or silk ribbon.

Figure 20
Leaves made with floral tape.

Figure 21
Taping lace leaves to a stem.

*Leaves made with silk ribbon*

Silk ribbon with an adhesive back can also be used to make leaves for any flower. The procedure is the same as described for the leaves made with contact paper.

*Floral tape leaves*

This material works particularly well for the leaves of the snowdrop, iris, daffodil, lily and orchid, because it lends itself to long shapes. It can also be used for other leaves.

Plate 1 ▶

*Leaves.* 1-6. Lace leaves. 1. Fuchsia. 2. Rose. 3. Daisy. 4. Wild pansy. 5. Snowdrop. 6. Forget-me-not. 7. Silk ribbon (2 sizes); can be adapted for any flower. 8. Floral tape; can be used for any long leaf. 9. Contact paper; cut to shape for a clematis leaf. 10. Silk florist leaves; can be used as they are or cut to any shape: *eg* fern is suitable for the orchid, the variegated leaf for the cyclamen, the very small leaf for the forget-me-not or any small flower, and the long leaf for the lily.

Cut twice the length of leaf required, place wire half-way along the tape. A little glue on the tape will help it to stick. Fold the tape over and press down (see Fig 20). Shape the top and bottom as shown, leaving a length of wire for the stem as required. Tape the stem. This type of leaf normally stands one to a stem and is added singly to the flower arrangement.

*Assembling lace leaves*
Join the leaves to the stem while the wire is being covered with floral tape. Hold the loose threads of the leaf to the wire and tape over the threads fixing them to the stem. The tape must be pulled tight round the wire to help hold the leaf in position (Fig 21; see also section on taping stems p 15).

*Assembling a spray with leaves made with contact paper, silk ribbon or worked in lace*
The main stem will be the longest and will bear one leaf at the top. To this you will add the side leaves made on shorter stalks (Fig 22). As the stalk is being taped down add in the side leaves on shorter stalks proceeding as you would for the lace leaves (explained above), but instead of pressing the loose threads to the main stem press the short wire stalk against the main stem and tape over (Fig 23).

*Natural leaves*
Natural leaves can be placed into preserving crystals for about two to three weeks. Follow instructions on container. When ready tape them to a wire stem and add to the arrangement.

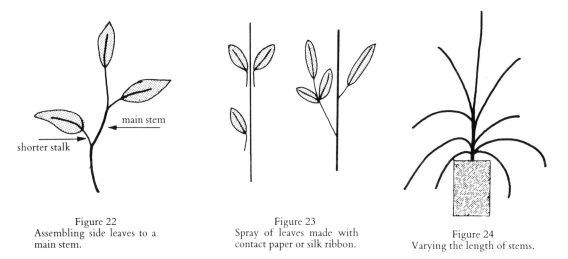

Figure 22
Assembling side leaves to a main stem.

Figure 23
Spray of leaves made with contact paper or silk ribbon.

Figure 24
Varying the length of stems.

## A note on the display of lace flower arrangements

When making the final display do not hesitate to bend and twist the petals, leaves and stems a little. This will give them a natural appearance. Also, try and vary the height of the stems. This will allow each of the flowers to stand out (Fig 24).

The correct choice of container or accessory is important in order to show off your arrangement to its best advantage. Small flowers look pretty in small containers such as baskets, wood or pottery pots, and small shells. Orchids lend themselves well to being displayed in deep set frames. Sprays of flowers such as forsythia, winter jasmine and japonica can be displayed, slightly curved, on plaques covered in velvet.

Arrangements placed in glass vases will not appear to their best advantage unless the taping of the stems is done with exceptional care.

Wild flowers like the poppy daisy or forget-me-not can be shown with small pieces of drift-wood.

A piece of slate, decorative stone or wood can be used as a base for a flower arrangement. Small pieces of dry foam (Oasis) or floral pack, as used by flower arrangers, can be glued to them to hold the flowers in position. Cover the base with leaves and set the flowers into it. Violets or primroses look attractive when displayed in this way. An empty cotton reel covered with a strip of lace can also be used to hold a spray.

## Suggestions for the use of lace flowers

Lace flowers can be used for a wedding instead of fresh flowers. A small silver vase with stems of freesia, lily, iris or a fuchsia could be placed on the top of the wedding cake to match the bride's lace flowered head-dress or corsage (button-hole) sprays.

Lace flowers make decorative objects just as flowers made from other materials such as porcelain or silver. For example: brooches, serviette rings, arrangements for display domes etc.

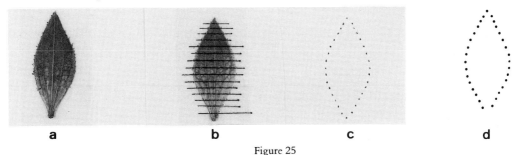

| a | b | c | d |

Figure 25

*Preparing a new pricking.* a. The natural petal or leaf is secured with transparent sticky tape. Several specimens are prepared and the best chosen for the next stage. b. Horizontal lines are drawn to determine the outlining pin-holes and the spacing between them, as well as the position of added pairs or any other features required. Here too several samples are made. c. The draft petal is pricked onto paper before being 'trued-up' onto card. d. The finished pricking.

## Designing your own lace flowers

Some readers may wish to go on further and design their own flowers. This is best done by studying the real flower. Figure 25 shows stages of preparation of a pricking for a new petal. When looking at a given specimen you should bear in mind the following questions: how many petals are there; what colour, texture and shape. How are they joined together, do they overlap? How many stamens can you see in the middle of each flower? Are there any veins, changes in colour? How does the flower-head join the main stem of the plant? If there are several flowers on one stalk how are they set in relation to each other; in a cluster, along one line (like the freesia), staggered or on facing points of a stem? Are some fully open and others in bud?

Then the leaves. What shape and what texture are they and how do they join onto the main stem? The more careful your study, the more detail and individuality you can give to your flowers.

The spray orchid on p 66 worked in red and silver lamé thread is intended as a Christmas corsage but can be made in other colour combinations and be worn as a brooch. The lamé ribbon (p 68) makes a good accessory for any arrangement.

# PART II THE FLOWERS

## FORSYTHIA

*Thread*    yellow 30 Mettler 500
*Stamens*   one small yellow
*Petals*    bud 2, flower 4
*Stitch*    cloth stitch, straight edges
*Symbols*   **x** starting point
*Leaves*    none required

INSTRUCTIONS
*The bud.* 10 pairs of bobbins. Make 2 petals.
*The flower.* 10 pairs of bobbins. Make 4 petals.

ASSEMBLY
*The bud.* Tie one stamen to the pad at the top of a short stem. Place the two petals facing each other, enclosing the stamen. Tie with a hitch knot and tape the stem.

*The flower.* Tie one stamen to the pad at the top of the stem. Add the four petals spaced evenly round the stamen tying them with a hitch knot one at a time. Tape the stem.

Make a number of flowers and buds on short wire stems not longer than $1\frac{1}{5}$ in (38 mm). Take a long wire, cover it with floral tape for about $\frac{1}{2}$ in (12 mm) then start adding the flowers in pairs on either side of the stem, making sure that only about $\frac{1}{2}$ in (12 mm) of the short stem remains visible. Wind the tape tightly round the short stem when attaching it to the main stem to hold the flowers securely in position.

When a flower stem is completed twist the petals a little by holding the tip between finger and thumb. If you look at the flowers of a forsythia you will see that its petals seem to twist and turn.

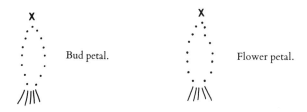

Bud petal.

Flower petal.

## SNOWDROP

*Thread*    white DMC 30 Retors d'Alsace; green 30 Mettler 540
*Stamens*    not required
*Petals*    inner 3, outer 3
*Stitch*    cloth stitch, straight edges
*Symbols*    **x**1, **x**2 starting points
*Leaves*    moss green long pointed leaves, made from floral tape or adhesive ribbon, or made in lace

## INSTRUCTIONS

*Inner petal.* 12 pairs of bobbins. The top part of the petal is worked in two halves with 5 pairs in white and 1 in green for each side.

Hang 4 passives and 1 weaver pair open on the starting pin **x**1, plus one green pair in the middle. Do the same for starting point **x**2. Work the left half to the left and the right half to the right (as indicated by the arrows) bringing the weavers to the centre. Work a cloth stitch, put in a pin; cover the pin with a cloth stitch (no twists). Drop one weaver down and make it a passive pair. Use the other weaver pair to work across. Working to the left follow the pattern until completed. Make 3 petals.

*Outer petals.* 10 pairs wound in white thread.

Hang pairs on starting pin **x** and work in cloth stitch through the pattern. Tie off as directed on p 13. Make 3 petals.

## ASSEMBLY

Cover the top of the wire with floral tape to make a pad (see p 14). This will make the single stamen. Place the inner petals round the base of the pad spacing them out equally. Tie each one in turn with a hitch knot. Add the outer petals making sure they cover up the gaps or spaces between the inner petals.

Tape the stem and bend the flower head a little to give it its characteristic appearance. Three or four flowers with four to five leaves are a minimum for this arrangement. Leaves can also be worked in lace, see p 69.

## COMMENT

If you make a number of snowdrops with a few long lace leaves and assemble them on one stem you would get the Summer Snowflake. Usually there are three flower-heads and about the same number of leaves to one stem.

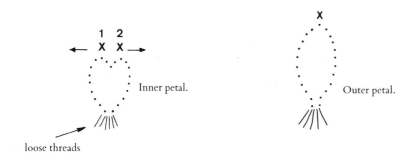

1 2
X X

Inner petal.

loose threads

X

Outer petal.

# CROCUS

*Thread*    large flower, purple 30 Mettler 583; small flower, gold 30 Mettler 828; brown 30 Mettler 528; leaves, green 30 Mettler 540; the stamens, gold Clark's Embroidery thread 0303

*Stamens*    3 lengths $\frac{3}{4}$ in (19 mm) of thread (all 6 strands)

*Petals*    bud 3, flower 6

*Stitch*    cloth stitch and half-stitch, straight edges

*Symbols*    **x** starting point; ● adding pairs on the edge; ∩ adding pairs in the centre

*Leaves*    long pointed ones in moss green, made from floral tape or adhesive silk ribbon; or worked in lace

## INSTRUCTIONS

*The large flower.* Work in purple thread. Wind 14 pairs of bobbins starting with 10 and adding 4, as shown. First work 5 rows in cloth stitch, then 6 rows in half-stitch and again 7 rows in cloth stitch. At the neck the cloth stitch will be packed tightly together and this will give the petal the necessary stiffness to hold its shape. Make 6 petals.

*The bud.* The petals for the bud are worked in purple thread, in the same manner as the flower. Make 3 petals.

*The small flower, inner petal.* Work in gold thread. Wind 14 pairs of bobbins; start with 10 and add 4 as indicated. First work 5 rows in cloth stitch, 6 rows in half-stitch and 6 rows in cloth stitch. Make 3 petals.

*The small flower, outer petal.* Work in gold and brown thread. Wind 11 pairs of bobbins in gold thread and 4 pairs of bobbins in brown. Work in cloth stitch throughout, adding the brown pairs, two to each inner pin-hole. Once you have added the brown pairs, the position of the pairs on the pricking will be as follows, from left to right: 4 gold, 2 brown, 2 gold, 2 brown, 4 gold plus the gold weaver. On reaching the neck of the petal leave out 2 pairs with gold thread, one at each inside edge. Make 6 petals.

## ASSEMBLY

*The bud.* Place three lengths of thread for the stamen against the pad at the top of the stem and tie with a hitch knot, using the same colour thread as that of the petals. Place the petals round the base of the stamens, spacing them out equally and tying each one in turn with a hitch knot. Tape the stem.

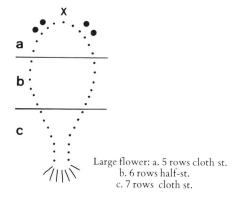

Large flower: a. 5 rows cloth st.
b. 6 rows half-st.
c. 7 rows cloth st.

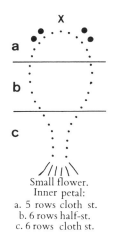

Small flower.
Inner petal:
a. 5 rows cloth st.
b. 6 rows half-st.
c. 6 rows cloth st.

Small flower
Outer petal.

24

*Continued overleaf* ▶

## WINTER JASMINE

*Thread*   yellow 30 Mettler 501
*Stamens*  one small yellow
*Petals*   bud 2, flower 6
*Stitch*   cloth stitch, straight edges
*Symbols*  **x** starting point; ⌡ hand-stitching
*Leaves*   none required

## INSTRUCTIONS

*The bud.* 8 pairs of bobbins. Leave out three pairs as you work down the neck. Make 2 petals.

*The flower.* 8 pairs of bobbins. Leave out three pairs as you work down the neck. Make 6 petals.

## ASSEMBLY

*The bud.* Tie one stamen to the pad at the top of the stem. Place the stamen between the two petals and stitch them one to another at the neck, making two seams enclosing the stamen. Leave on a short stem and tape.

*The flower.* Prepare a stamen as above. Stitch the six petals one to another at the neck and then insert the stamen down the tube. See Fig 18, p 15. Tie with a hitch knot and tape.

Make a number of flowers and buds on short wire stems not longer than $1\frac{1}{2}$ in 38 mm). Take a long wire and cover it with floral tape for about $\frac{1}{2}$ in (12 mm). Start adding the flowers and buds in pairs opposite each other leaving a $\frac{3}{4}$ in (19 mm) gap between each pair, taping as you go. Make sure that no more than $\frac{3}{4}$ in (19 mm) of the short stem remains visible and that you wind the floral tape tightly round the short and the main stem, as this will hold the flowers securely in position. In order to achieve the slightly ridged appearance of the winter jasmine petals, press the outer edges of each petal together as shown on the photo opposite.

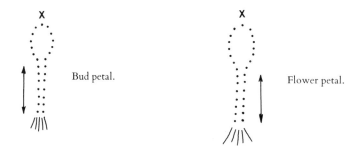

Bud petal.

Flower petal.

*Continued from page 24.*

*The flower.* Assemble as for the bud adding the three additional petals on the outside, making sure that they cover the space between the inner petals. Tie each with a hitch knot and tape the stem.

*The leaves.* Aim to obtain a leaf 4 in (10 cm) long by $\frac{3}{8}$ in (9.5 cm) wide.

## COMMENT

Assemble the smaller golden-brown flower in the same way as the larger one, but make sure that the petal with the brown stripe is on the outside. Group two to three crocuses together and surround them by at least four leaves to complete the arrangement.

## PRIMROSE

| | |
|---|---|
| *Thread* | yellow 30 Mettler 502 |
| *Stamen* | one small yellow |
| *Petals* | bud 2, flower 5 |
| *Stitch* | half stitch, straight edges |
| *Symbols* | **x** starting point |
| *Leaves* | silk leaves or adhesive ribbon, mid or moss green as available |

## INSTRUCTIONS

*The bud.* 12 pairs of bobbins. The top part of the petal is worked in two stages.

Hang 6 pairs on each starting pin (marked **x**1, **x**2) and work the left half to the left and the right half to the right (as indicated by the arrows), bringing the two weavers to the centre. Work a cloth stitch, put in a pin and cover the pin with a cloth stitch (no twists). Drop down one of the weaver pairs to become a passive, using the other to work across until it is completed. Make 2 petals.

*The flower.* Follow the above instructions and make 5 petals.

## ASSEMBLY

*The bud.* Tie one stamen to the pad at the top of the stem. Place the two petals facing each other and enclosing the stamen. Tie with a hitch knot and tape the stem. Curl one petal round the other to form a tight bud.

*The flower.* Tie one stamen to the pad at the top of the stem. Add the five petals one by one, each overlapping the previous petal a little and tying each with a hitch knot in turn. Tape the stem. When the flower is made up, gently curl the edge of the petal to give it its typical shape (see photo opposite).

*Leaves.* Follow the pattern to cut out the leaves, varying the size. Silk leaves already have a stem. For silk ribbon leaves follow the instructions on p 16.

## COMMENTS

The primroses look particularly attractive arranged in a little basket-like container. Glue a small piece of dry foam (Oasis) to the bottom of the container to hold the flowers. The leaves should be arranged so as to cover the dry foam.

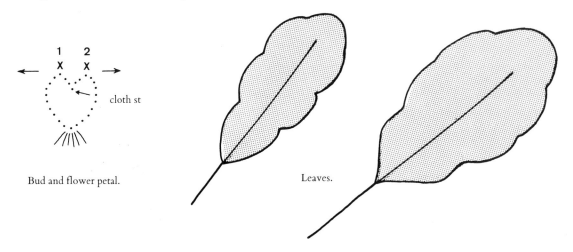

Bud and flower petal.

cloth st

Leaves.

## DAFFODIL

*Thread* white DMC 30 Retors d'Alsace; yellow 30 Mettler 500; gold 30 Mettler 828; leaves, green 30 Mettler 540

*Stamens* one long yellow, two small yellow

*Petals* bud 4 and 1 trumpet, flower 6 and 1 trumpet

*Stitch* cloth stitch and cloth stitch with twists on the weavers, half- stitch, straight and serrated edges

*Symbols* **x** starting point, • adding pairs, ⌡ hand-stitching

*Leaves* moss green, long lance-like leaves made from floral tape or adhesive silk ribbon; or lace leaves

## INSTRUCTIONS

*The trumpet.* This is worked in two stages. Start with the frill in cloth stitch (arrow 1) with 6 pairs of bobbins. Work a serrated edge on the outer edge of the frill. On the inside edge add one pair of bobbins to every pin-hole (15 pairs in all). Work only until point A. Leave the 6 pairs of the frill in abeyance and turn the pillow round; work part 2 (arrow 2) in half-stitch. At the base of the trumpet tie off threads at the pin-holes marked on the pricking.

Return to the frill and work parts 3 and 4 (see arrows) in the same order. Hand stitch the sides of the trumpet as indicated.

*The petals (two possible methods).*

A. Work with 10 pairs of bobbins, 2 rows of cloth stitch, 2 rows with two twists on the weavers before working the passive pairs, 5 rows with three twists on the weavers; complete with 2 rows of cloth stitch as shown by lines on the pricking. Make 4 for a bud and 6 for a flower.

B. Work entirely in cloth stitch. Start with 12 pairs, adding one pair at each point marked • (making 20 pairs in all).

## ASSEMBLY

*The bud.* Tie one long and two short stamens to the pad at the top of the stem. Insert the stem half way down into the prepared trumpet (see also p 15). Tie with a hitch knot. Place four petals evenly round the trumpet tying each in turn.

*The flower.* Tie one long stamen and two short ones to the pad at the top of the stem. Insert the stem half way down into the prepared trumpet (see also p 15) and tie with a hitch knot. Place and tie 3 petals evenly round the trumpet. Add the outer petals making sure that they cover up the gaps between the inner petals. Tape the stem.

Every flower requires at least two leaves.

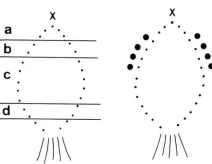

Method A: a. 2 rows cloth st.
b. 2 rows cloth st & 2 twists.
c. 5 rows cloth st & 3 twist.
d. 2 rows cloth st.

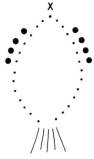

Method B.

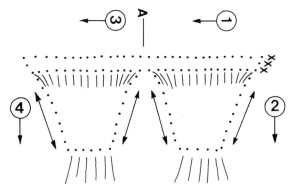

Trumpet.

## DAISY

| | |
|---|---|
| *Thread* | small flower, white DMC 30 Retors d'Alsace; large flower, colours of your own choice in sewing cotton; leaves, green 30 Mettler 549 |
| *Stamen* | small flower, one large round yellow; large flower, one or more to match the colour of the petals |
| *Petals* | small flower, inner circle 6, outer circle 6; large flower, 5 |
| *Stitch* | cloth stitch, straight edges |
| *Symbols* | **x** starting point |
| *Leaves* | made in lace |

## INSTRUCTIONS

*Small flower.* 6 pairs of bobbins. Make 6 petals for the inner circle and 6 for the outer circle.

*Large flower.* 8 pairs of bobbins. Make 5 or more petals.

*Leaf.* 10 pairs of bobbins. Work in cloth stitch with straight edges. In order to vary the texture of the leaves work a ladder pattern on some of them (see p 12 and leaf for the Canary bird rose).

## ASSEMBLY

*Small flower.* Tie the stamen to the pad at the top of the stem. Spread the 6 petals evenly round the stamen, tying them one at a time. This will form the inner ring of petals. Repeat this for the outer circle. Tape the stem. Gently curl the petals curving them slightly outwards.

*Large flower.* Start as above and add the five (or more) petals, tying them in turn with a hitch knot and making sure that they are evenly spaced round either one, four or five stamens, as appropriate.

*Leaf.* Tie the thread ends securely to the pad at the top of a short wire stem. Tape the stem, making sure that the thread ends are well covered.

Make up the small daisies on short stems (daisies only grow to a small height). As a guide you can assemble four flowers with three leaves, which will make a compact arrangement to fit an egg cup or small basket. You could also make one or two of the flowers with petals on only one side of the stamen. This will make it look as if it is fading, giving a extra natural dimension to the arrangement.

## COMMENT

The large flower with 5 petals, or more, is a 'made-up' one, see Plate 3 p 39. An arrangement of 4 to 5 of these large 'daisies' in the colour of your choice can be assembled into a corsage spray.

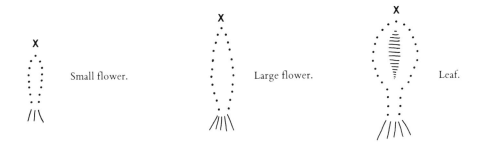

Small flower.  Large flower.  Leaf.

## JAPONICA

| | |
|---|---|
| *Thread* | red 30 Mettler 921; orange 30 Mettler 822; white DMC 30 Retors d'Alsace; yellow sewing cotton, approximately 1 yard (91 cm) long for the tufted stamen |
| *Stamens* | one green with a tuft of yellow cotton (see p 14) |
| *Petals* | small bud 3, medium size flower 5, large flower 5 |
| *Stitch* | cloth stitch, cloth stitch with two twists on the weavers; straight edges |
| *Symbols* | **x** starting point, ● adding pairs |
| *Leaves* | not required, but can be added at the base of the arrangement (see photo opposite) |

### INSTRUCTIONS

*The bud.* 10 pairs wound with the colour of your choice. Make 3 petals in cloth stitch.

*Medium-size flower.* 10 pairs. Make 5 petals in cloth stitch, with one twist on the weaver.

*Large flower.* Start with 10 pairs and add one at each point marked ● (12 in all). Make 5 petals in cloth stitch, with two twists on the weaver.

### ASSEMBLY

*The bud.* Tie one tuft stamen to the pad at the top of a stem. Place the three petals evenly round the stamen and tie them with a hitch knot. Leave on a short (1½ in, 38 cm) stem and tape.

*Medium size and large flower.* These are assembled in the same way as the bud except that five petals have to be evenly spaced round the stamen and tied. Leave on short stems and tape.

Make up a number of buds and flowers. Take a long wire, tape about ¾ in (19 mm) down the wire then start adding in the buds and flowers in clusters, taping as you work down (see photo opposite). The tape will hold the buds and flowers in position.

Bud petal.

Medium flower petal.

Larger flower petal.

34

## NARCISSUS

| | |
|---|---|
| *Thread* | gold 30 Mettler 828; white 30 DMC Retors d'Alsace; leaves, green 30 Mettler 549 |
| *Stamen* | two yellow |
| *Petals* | inner petals 3, outer petals 3, and 1 trumpet |
| *Stitch* | cloth stitch and half-stitch, straight edges |
| *Symbols* | **x** starting point, • adding pairs, ↑ hand-stitching |
| *Leaves* | moss green, lance-like, made from floral tape or adhesive silk ribbon, or worked in lace |

## INSTRUCTIONS

*The trumpet.* Each half of the trumpet is worked separately. Hang 2 pairs, in gold, on each pin-hole (20 pairs in all) and work in half-stitch to the base. Tie off at the base. Make two halves and hand sew along lines indicated on the pricking.

*Inner petals.* Start with 10 pairs in white and add one at each point marked • (14 in all). Work in cloth stitch. Make 3 petals in cloth stitch.

*Outer petals.* Start with 10 pairs in white and add one pair at each point marked • (16 in all). Make 3 in cloth stitch.

## ASSEMBLY

*The flower.* Tie two stamens to the pad at the top of the stem. Insert the stem half-way down the prepared trumpet. Place three petals evenly round the stamens and the trumpet, and tie each one in turn with a hitch knot. Add the three outer petals making sure that they cover the gaps between the inner petals. Tape the stem.

*The leaves.* At least three leaves are needed for each flower in this arrangement.

## COMMENT

To give the flower its realistic appearance gently pinch together the tip of each petal, forming a short groove (see photo opposite).

If you wish to make a bud proceed as for the flower but instead of spreading out the petals, push them together.

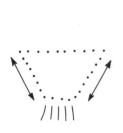

Trumpet.

Inner petal.

Outer petal.

Plate 2
*From left to right, back row*: Poppy, Canary bird rose, Narcissus, Japonica. *Foreground and centre*: Silver orchid corsage, Iris, Wild pansy, Daffodil.

## VIOLET

| | |
|---|---|
| *Thread* | white DMC 30 Retors d'Alsace; purple 30 Mettler 583; mauve 30 Mettler 577 |
| *Stamen* | one small yellow |
| *Petals* | 5 |
| *Stitch* | cloth stitch, straight edges |
| *Symbols* | **x** starting point |
| *Leaves* | cut from silk leaves or natural leaves preserved in crystals |

## INSTRUCTIONS

*Top petal.* 8 pairs of bobbins. Make 2 petals.

*Side petal.* 6 pairs of bobbins. Make 2 petals.

*Bottom petal.* 10 pairs of bobbins. Make one petal.

   As you complete each petal pin them on your pillow following the pattern layout, as shown, otherwise it may be difficult to distinguish one from the other when coming to make up the flower.

## ASSEMBLY

Tie one stamen to the pad at the top of the stem, and tie the front lip petal (No 5) to it, followed by the two side petals (3 & 4). Attach the two top petals (1 & 2) last. Tape the stem.

   A bunch of violets made in different colours looks very pretty when arranged in a small pottery vase, a basket or a tiny piece of drift-wood covered with moss. Remember to vary the heights of the stems for flowers and leaves.

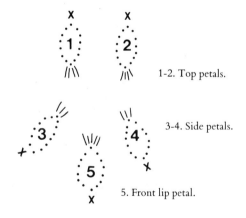

1-2. Top petals.

3-4. Side petals.

5. Front lip petal.

Plate 3

◀ *From left to right, back row*: Winter jasmine, Violet, Fuchsia, 'Made-up' large daisy, Lily. *Foreground and centre*: Daisy, Crocus, Forsythia, Garden cyclamen.

## IRIS

*Thread*   white DMC 30 Retors d'Alsace; blue 30 Mettler 498; yellow 30 Mettler 500; leaves, green 30 Mettler 549; gimp, yellow DMC Fil à dentelles 743

*Stamens*   3 small long yellow

*Petals*   bud 3; flower, inner 3 and outer 3

*Stitch*   cloth stitch and half-stitch; straight edges

*Symbols*   **x** starting point; • adding pairs at the edge; ⋒ adding pairs in the centre of the petal

*Leaves*   green, long and slim, made from floral tape, adhesive ribbon, cut to shape from silk leaves or made in lace

## INSTRUCTIONS

*The bud.* 10 pairs, add 1 pair at each point marked (14 in all). Work in cloth stitch. Make 3 petals.

*The flower*

*Inner petal.* 10 pairs wound with coloured thread of your choice. Make 3 in half-stitch.

*Outer petal.* Start with 11 pairs adding one at each pin-hole marked • (15 in all). At the centre pin-hole separate the bobbins, 7 to one side and 8 to the other (the latter will contain the weaver). Put in pin, hang on the yellow gimp.

■ † Starting from the left-hand edge (see working diagram) work through 6 pairs (including the edge stitch); twist the weaver twice, pass the gimp through the weaver pair and twist the weaver twice again. Work the next two pairs in cloth stitch, twist the weaver twice, pass the gimp through the weaver, twist the weaver twice again, work the 6 pairs to the right-hand edge in cloth stitch.†

Repeat from † to † three times before crossing over the gimp.

Cross the gimp threads over each other, left over right (see working diagram).■

Repeat ■ to ■ five times for each petal.

When you reach the neck of the petal continue working in cloth stitch keeping the yellow gimp as passive pair threads and leaving out 4 pairs of the main colour. This will give a neat appearance to the petal. Make 3 petals.

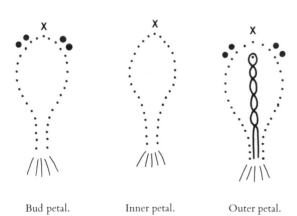

Bud petal.          Inner petal.          Outer petal.

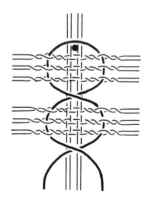

Working diagram for gimp.

*Continued overleaf* ▶

## GARDEN CYCLAMEN

*Thread*    white and shades of pink in sewing cotton
*Stamen*   one small long yellow
*Petals*    bud 3, flower 5
*Stitch*    cloth stitch, straight edges
*Symbols*  **x** starting point; ⌡ hand-stitching
*Leaves*   variegated silk leaves or natural leaves dried in preserving crystals

## INSTRUCTIONS

*The bud.* 10 pairs of bobbins. Make 3 petals.

*The flower.* 10 pairs of bobbins. Make 5 petals.

## ASSEMBLY

*The bud.* Tie one stamen to the pad at the top of a short stem. Hand stitch together the three neck edges of the petals as indicated on the pattern by the arrows, making three seams in all to form the tube. Insert the stamen into the tube so that only the tip of the stamen protrudes from the tube. Tie with a hitch knot. Tape the stem. Hold the tips of the three petals together and twist as one.

*The flower.* Proceed as for a bud, except that you need to stitch the necks of five petals together (making five seams in all). Insert the stamen and tie with a hitch knot at the base of the tube. Tape the stem. When the flower is assembled turn back the petals as required for a cyclamen (see photo opposite).

## COMMENT

You could add a twisted stem to represent a seed head for extra decoration. Work as follows. Cover a length of wire with floral tape and twist it round a thin knitting needle to make a fine spiral. Place this in with the flowers.

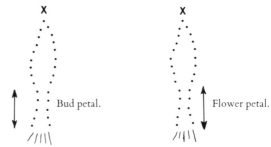

Bud petal.    Flower petal.

---

*Continued from page 42.*

## ASSEMBLY

*The bud.* Tie the three stamens to the pad. Place the three petals evenly round the stamens; tie and tape.

*The flower.* Tie three stamens to the pad. Place the three **outer** petals evenly round the stamens and tie. Then put each of the three **inner** petals in the spaces between the outer ones, tying as you work. Tape the stem. To shape the Iris bring the tips of the three inner petals together in the centre. It may be necessary to add a dab of glue to the tips of the inner petals to hold them in position. Then curve the three outside petals downwards (see photo).

## WILD PANSY

*Thread*    flower, purple 30 Mettler 583; yellow 30 Mettler 501; leaves, green 30 Mettler 549
*Stamen*    one small yellow
*Petals*    5
*Stitch*    petals, cloth stitch; straight edges; leaves, cloth stitch serrated edges
*Symbols*   **x** starting point
*Leaves*    worked in lace

## INSTRUCTIONS

*Petals 1 & 2, top petals.* 10 pairs of bobbins wound in purple.

*Petals 3 & 4, side petals.* 8 Pairs of bobbins wound in yellow.

*Petal 5, front lip petal.* 10 pairs of bobbins wound in yellow.

*Leaves.* 10 pairs of bobbins wound in green thread. Work in cloth stitch with a serrated edge, see p 12. In order to vary the texture, work a ladder pattern following instructions on p 12 and details for the leaf of the Canary bird rose.

## ASSEMBLY

*The flower.* Tie one stamen to the pad at the top of a medium length stem. To this you first tie (with a hitch knot) the side petals Nos 3 & 4, followed by the top petals Nos 1 & 2 and finally the front lip petal No 5. Tape the stem.

   This sequence of assembly is very important to the natural look of the finished flower.

*The leaf.* Place the end threads of the leaf against the pad of a short stem and tape over to anchor the leaf in position. Continue taping down the stem.

## COMMENT

The wild pansy looks good combined with a few daisies and dried grasses.

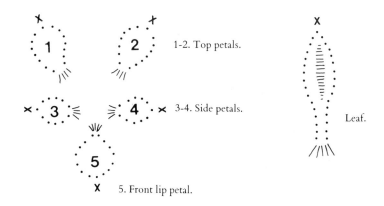

1-2. Top petals.

3-4. Side petals.

5. Front lip petal.

Leaf.

## FORGET-ME-NOT

| | |
|---|---|
| *Thread* | flower, shades of blue, 30 Mettler 788, 498; leaves, green 30 Mettler 540 |
| *Stamen* | one small yellow |
| *Petals* | bud 2, flower 5 |
| *Stitch* | cloth stitch, straight edges |
| *Symbols* | **x** starting point |
| *Leaves* | made in lace or with silk leaves |

## INSTRUCTIONS

*The bud.* 6 pairs of bobbins. Make 2 petals.

*The flower.* 6 pairs of bobbins. Make 5 petals.

*The leaf.* 8 pairs of bobbins wound with green thread. Make at least 4 leaves in cloth stitch.

## ASSEMBLY

*The bud.* Tie one stamen to the pad at the top of a long stem. Place the stamen between two petals. Tie with a hitch knot and leave till the final assembly.

*The flower.* Tie one stamen to the pad at the top of a short stem. Arrange five petals round the stamen, tying each one with a hitch knot. Tape the stem.

## FINAL ASSEMBLY

Prepare several buds and a number of flowers. Start by taping the long stem holding the bud. Add more buds and then flowers, staggering them as you continue taping down the stem. Leave as small a gap between the flowers and buds as possible. Towards the base of the stem incorporate a few leaves. These will not require stems of their own but can be attached to the main stem by securing the loose threads with the tape (see also section on assembling lace leaves p 18). The petals of this flower are delicate to make but the flower is pretty when finished.

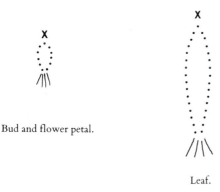

Bud and flower petal.

Leaf.

## POPPY

*Thread* flower and bud, red Mettler 600; bud, green Mettler 540
*Stamens* bud, 1 large yellow; flower, 1 large yellow and about 12 small green
*Petals* bud 4, flower (small or large) 4
*Stitch* cloth stitch, cloth stitch with twists on the weavers, straight edges
*Symbols* **x** starting point, ● adding pairs, ↑ hand-stitching
*Leaves* use dried grasses or natural leaves preserved in crystals

## INSTRUCTIONS

*Bud.* 10 pairs of bobbins. Work in cloth stitch. Make 2 in green and 2 in red.

*Small flower.* Wind 16 pairs. Start working with 10, then add one at each pin-hole marked on the pricking (16 in all). Work the first four rows in cloth stitch. Then work a ladder effect by twisting the weavers at the centre of the petal, first twice then progressively to four twists. Decrease the number of twists as pattern narrows. See also instructions for ladder effect p 12. Make 4 petals.

*Large flower.* Wind 24 pairs. Start with 10 on each point marked **x** and add 2 pairs on each side. Work both sides in cloth stitch for four rows, the left half to the left and the right half to the right. Work a straight edge.
Bring the weavers from both sides to the centre (see working diagram). Join the weavers with a cloth stitch, put in pin, and work another cloth stitch. Continue working each half from the edge to the centre, joining the weavers each time they meet at the centre, as above. Follow the pricking, tailing off into two halves. Make 4 petals.

## ASSEMBLY

*Bud.* Tie one stamen to the pad at the top of the stem. Place the two red petals facing each other, enclosing the stamen. Add the two green petals, also facing each other, to overlap the gaps between the two red petals. Tie each petal with a hitch knot. Tape the stem.

*Small and large flower.* Draw black stripes on the large yellow stamen. Tie it to the pad at the top of the stem; surround with the small stamens. Mark the base of the petals with a black felt tip pen as shown on the photograph and the colour Plate, p 38. Arrange the petals evenly round the stamens and tie with a hitch knot. Tape the stem.

Before assembling the large flower, sew the two inner edges of the base together by hand, as indicated. This will give the petal a cupped effect.

## COMMENT

Dried poppy seed heads and dried grass look attractive with this arrangement.

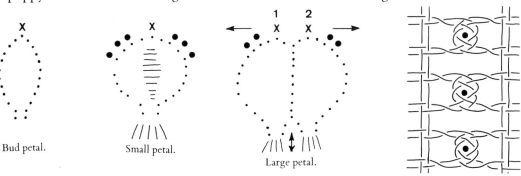

Bud petal.

Small petal.

Large petal.

Working diagram for the joining of weavers.

## FUCHSIA

*Thread*    deep pink 30 Mettler 835; purple 30 Mettler 583; white 30 DMC Retors d'Alsace; leaves, green 30 Mettler 549

*Stamen*    6 small black

*Petals*    small bud 3, medium size bud 3; flower, inner petals 3, outer petals 4

*Stitch*    petals and leaves, cloth stitch, straight edges

*Symbols*    **x** starting point

*Leaves*    4 to a stem, worked in lace

### INSTRUCTIONS

*Small bud.* 6 pairs. Make 3 petals.

*Medium size bud.* 8 pairs. Make 3 petals. When choosing the colour for the buds bear in mind that it should match the colour of the outer petals of the flower.

*Flower.* The inner petals, 10 pairs. Make 3 petals. Outer petals, 10 pairs. Make 4 petals.

*Leaf.* 10 pairs. To vary the texture of the leaf work three to four twists on the weavers in the centre, starting from the third row. This will achieve a ladder effect. See also p 12, and the leaf for the Canary bird rose.

### ASSEMBLY

When preparing the stamens for either bud or flower make sure that they vary in length and in particular that one is clearly a little longer than the others (see photo opposite).

*The bud.* Tie the cluster of stamens to the pad at the top of the stem. Evenly space the petals round the stamens, tie with a hitch knot and tape.

*The flower.* Prepare the stamens as above and place the 3 inner petals evenly round the stamens; tie with a hitch knot. Place the 4 outer petals, 2 at a time opposite each other, tying each pair in turn with a hitch knot. Tape the stem. Curl back the four outer petals to give the flower its correct shape.

*The spray.* To assemble a spray put one bud on a long wire; do **not** tape it yet. Tie the remaining buds and flowers to shorter wires of various lengths and tape them. Then tape the bud on the long wire including further buds, flowers and leaves as you tape down the stem. The lace leaves do not need a wire stem. You can anchor them to the main stem by taping over the $\frac{1}{2}$ in (13 mm) long threads at the base of the leaf, directly onto the main stem.

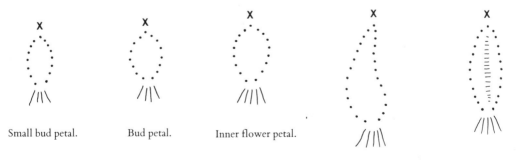

Small bud petal.    Bud petal.    Inner flower petal.

Outer flower petal.    Leaf.

## CANARY BIRD ROSE

*Thread*     bright yellow 30 Mettler 501; leaves, green 30 Mettler 540; tufted stamen, gold 30 Mettler 828

*Stamen*     1 stamen and 1 tuft made with gold coloured cotton

*Petals*     bud 2, flower 5

*Stitch*     petals, half-stitch, straight edges; leaves, cloth stitch with ladder effect, serrated edges

*Symbols*     **x** starting point

*Leaves*     silk leaves or worked in lace.

## INSTRUCTIONS

*Bud and flower.* 16 pairs, 8 pairs at each starting point. Work five rows in half-stitch, one half to the left and the other to the right as shown by the arrows. Bring in the two weavers to the centre. Work a cloth stitch. Drop one weaver down to become a passive pair and use the other to keep working the petal in half-stitch to the base. Make 2 petals for the bud and 5 for the flower.

*The leaf.* 12 pairs. Start with 10 and add 2, as indicated. Work in cloth stitch, and serrated edge. Add ladder effect starting from the third row in the centre. Twist the weavers from 2 to 4 times and then decrease to 2 again, see p 12. Make five leaves for each spray.

## ASSEMBLY

*Bud.* Tie a small stamen to the pad at the top of the stem. One petal curled on itself will make a small bud. Two petals rolled round each other will make a slightly larger bud. Start from the top where you will have the smallest bud on the longest stem. Do not tape but leave aside and prepare several other buds on slightly shorter stems and tape these.

*The flower.* Flowers are assembled on shorter stems than buds. Start by making the tufted stamen as shown on p 14. Around this stamen place 5 petals and tie each with a hitch knot.

*The leaves.* Tie one leaf to a pad at the top of a long stem; do **not** tape it yet. Tie the remaining leaves to shorter stems and tape them. Then tape the leaf on the long wire including further leaves as you work down the stem to obtain the characteristic rose leaf formation.

*Final assembly.* Start by taping the small bud on the longest stem, adding buds, leaves and flower heads as you tape down the stem.

## COMMENT

This pattern worked in pink thread will make a lovely wild rose.

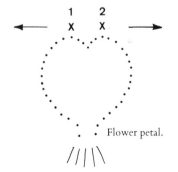

Flower petal.

Leaf.

## CLEMATIS MONTANA

*Thread*   pink lilac Sylko sewing cotton D440; cream sewing cotton approximately 1 yard (91 cm)
*Stamen*   1 stamen and a tuft
*Petals*   bud 2, flower 4
*Stitch*   cloth stitch, straight edges
*Symbols*  **x** starting point, ● adding pairs, ↕ hand-stitching
*Leaves*   green contact paper

## INSTRUCTIONS

*The bud.* 10 pairs of bobbins; add 2 pairs. Make 2 petals.

*The flower.* 10 pairs of bobbins, add 2 pairs. Make 4 petals.

## ASSEMBLY

*The bud.* Tie one stamen to the pad at the top of a long stem. Surround this with the cream tuft, spreading it evenly, and tie with a hitch knot. Place between two petals of the bud and tie each petal in turn with a hitch knot. Hand sew the edges of the petals half way on each side. This is to keep the bud in shape. Leave to one side without taping. Also, make several buds on short stems.

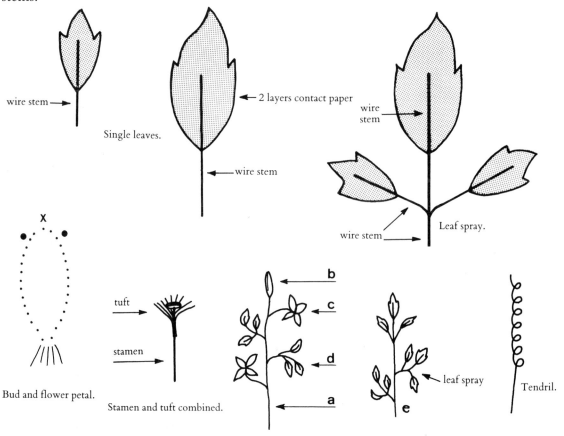

wire stem →

Single leaves.

← 2 layers contact paper

wire stem

← wire stem

wire stem →

Leaf spray.

**x**

Bud and flower petal.

tuft →

stamen →

Stamen and tuft combined.

b
c
d
a

leaf spray

e

Tendril.

Combined spray: a. Main stem.
b. Bud on main stem.
c. Flower. d. Leaf spray.
e. Assembled leaf arrangement.

*Continued overleaf* ▶

## LILY

*Thread*    yellow 30 Mettler 500; orange 30 Mettler 829 or 953; leaves, green 30 Mettler 540
*Stamens*    1 long and 4 small, yellow
*Petals*    bud 4, flower 6
*Stitch*    cloth stitch, cloth stitch with two twists on the weavers, straight edges
*Symbols*    **x** starting point
*Leaves*    long and thin, can be made from floral tape or cut from silk leaves, or made in lace

## INSTRUCTIONS

*The bud.* 10 pairs. Work three rows in cloth stitch, then change to cloth stitch with two twists on the weavers before working each passive pair. Work to the base of the petal and tie off. Make 4 petals.

*The flower.* 12 pairs. Work first four rows in cloth stitch then change to cloth stitch with two twists on the weavers. Work to the base of the petal and tie off. Make 6 petals.

## ASSEMBLY

*The bud.* Tie the stamens to the pad. Place the petals evenly round the stamen and tie one at a time. Curl the petals around each other. Tape the stem.

*The flower.* Tie the stamens as above. First place three petals evenly around the stamens and tie. Put the remaining three over the spaces left between the first three. Tape the stem. Shape the petals by curving them lightly out and downwards.

## COMMENT

For a flower arrangement you need to tie the bud to a longer stem (see photo, opposite). Vary the height of the flower stems. Hold the base of the stems and leaves in one hand and tape them together with floral tape. This will hold them together so that they can easily be put into a slender pottery or wooden vase.

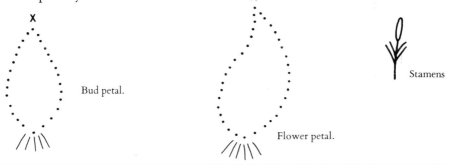

Bud petal.

Flower petal.

Stamens

---

*Continued from page 56.*

*The flower.* Assemble the stamen as above and place the four petals round it one at a time, tying each with a hitch knot. Leave on a short stem and tape. Make up several flowers.

*Leaves.* Follow the patterns (p 56), and instructions on p 16. Make up on a short stem and tape. A few leaves could be prepared on long stems and taped.

*Making a spray.* Take the long bud stem, start taping under the bud as explained on p 15 and work in the made up flowers and leaves while taping down the stem as shown in the assembly diagram. If you wish you could add tendrils by following the instructions on p 44.

## FREESIA

*Thread*    mauve 30 Mettler 577; yellow 30 Mettler 502; white 30 DMC Retors d'Alsace; leaves, green 30 Mettler 540; stamens, yellow Clark's embroidery thread 0298 (all 6 strands)

*Stamens*    6 lengths of thread $\frac{3}{4}$ in (19 mm) long

*Petals*    bud 1, flower 3

*Stitch*    half-stitch, cloth stitch, straight edges

*Symbols*    **x** starting point, ↧ hand-stitching

*Leaves*    floral tape or worked in lace

### INSTRUCTIONS

*The bud and flower.* 16 pairs, 8 on each starting point. Work the left half in half-stitch and the right half in cloth stitch until the horizontal line. When you reach the line bring the two weavers to the centre, drop one weaver to become a passive pair and use the other to continue working, in cloth stitch only, to the end, leaving out four pairs on the way. Make one petal for the bud and three for the flower.

To form the tube of the flower, hand sew the edges of the petals to one another along the line shown on the pricking.

### ASSEMBLY

Flowers and buds need to be on short stems. At the very top there will be green buds made with floral tape, then one or two lace buds and finally the open flowers (see photo).

*Green bud.* Cover a short length of wire with floral tape, thickening the top to form a bud-like shape. Make three or four of these.

*The lace bud.* Hand-sew together the sides of one petal. Take 6 lengths, $\frac{3}{4}$ in (19 mm) long, of Clark's embroidery thread (use all 6 strands), bunch them together and tie them to the pad at the top of a stem (Fig 14) to form a tuft. Take the tuft half way down the tube as shown on Fig 18 and tie tightly at the base of the tube. Make one or two buds.

*The flower.* Hand sew the sides of three petals, one section to the next, as indicated on the pricking. Make the stamen as for the bud, take down the tube as directed above and tie with a hitch knot at the base. Make several flower heads.

*Making up the spray.* Cover the top of a long wire with several turns of floral tape. Tape down the stem adding in, at about $\frac{3}{4}$ in (19 mm) intervals, green buds, then lace buds and finally the open flower heads. When complete bend the stem to form a curve.

*Leaves.* Make long thin leaves from floral tape, or cut from silk ones.

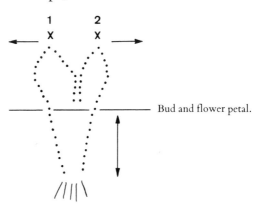

Bud and flower petal.

61

## ORCHID 1

*Thread*     cream 30 Mettler 502; colour veining and lip petal, gold 30 Mettler 517
*Stamens*   one very small yellow
*Petals*      5
*Stitch*      cloth stitch, half-stitch, straight edges
*Symbols*   **x** starting point, • adding pairs, ⋂ adding pairs in the centre of petal
*Leaves*     floral tape or silk fern

## INSTRUCTIONS

*The flower.* Four different shapes of petals make up the orchid. Pin each finished petal onto the pillow, following the numbers on the pattern. This will help in the assembly of the flower.

Start with petal No 3. 12 pairs worked in cloth stitch.

Petals 2 & 4: start with 10 pairs and work in cloth stitch. When you reach the pin-holes in the centre marked ⋂ put up a pin in each of the pin-holes shown and hang a pair of the different colour on each pin. Work to the base and tie off.

Petals 1 & 5: start with 10 pairs and work in cloth stitch. At the pin-holes marked ⋂ hang in 4 additional pairs of a different colour.

Petal 6: start with 12 pairs and work in half-stitch. Add 4 pairs at the edges, as indicated.

## ASSEMBLY

Tie one small stamen to the pad at the top of a stem. Lay it on petal No 6. Join the base of the petal with a sewing stitch. This will make the petal curl round the stamen. Tie petal No 3 to this, then Nos 2 & 4, followed by Nos 1 & 5. Tape the stem. Bear in mind that the order in which the petals are tied together is crucial to the final appearance of the flower.

*Leaves.* Long slim leaves can be made from floral tape, adhesive ribbon or cut out from silk fern.

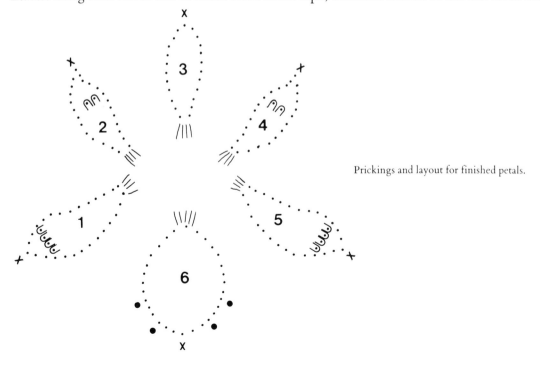

Prickings and layout for finished petals.

## ORCHID 2

*Thread*    purple 30 Mettler 583, mauve 577
*Stamen*    one small yellow
*Stitch*    cloth stitch, half-stitch, straight edges
*Symbols*   **x** starting point, ● adding pairs
*Leaves*    floral tape, adhesive backed ribbon, silk fern

### INSTRUCTIONS

*The flower.* Four different shapes of petals make up this orchid. Pin each finished petal onto the pillow, following the numbers on the pattern. This will help in the assembly of the flower. The combination of colour is a matter for personal choice; the flower pictured here has petals 4, 5 & 6 in the darker shade.

Start with petals 1,2 & 3. Set in 12 pairs and add 2 pairs on each side as indicated by ●. Work in cloth stitch.

Petals 4 & 5: start with 10 pairs and add 2 on each side as indicated, working in half-stitch.

Petal 6 (front lip petal): start with 12 pairs and add 2 on each side as shown. Work in half-stitch.

### ASSEMBLY

Tie a small stamen to the pad at the top of a stem with a hitch knot. Place it between petals Nos 6 & 2 and tie with a hitch knot. Add petal 4 & 5 on either side of petal No 2. Then tie in Nos 1 & 3 on either side of petal No 6., as shown on the layout.

*Leaves.* Long lance-like leaves can be made from floral tape, adhesive-backed ribbon, or cut out from pieces of silk fern.

### COMMENT

Orchids add a festive look to a garment. Also to a gift box where you can tone in or contrast the wrapping paper with the shades of the flower.

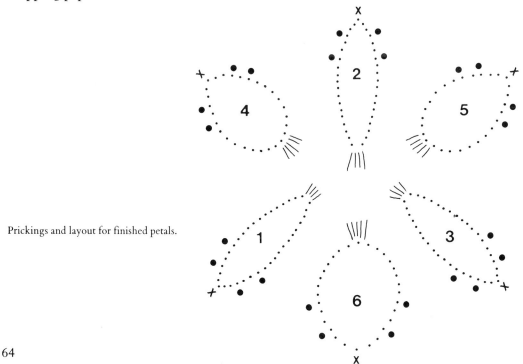

Prickings and layout for finished petals.

## SILVER ORCHID CORSAGE

| | |
|---|---|
| *Thread* | silver and red lamé DMC 10 Fil d'Argent à broder |
| *Stamens* | 2 small red |
| *Petals* | 4 |
| *Stitch* | cloth stitch, straight edges |
| *Symbols* | **x** starting point, ∩ adding pairs in the centre of the petal |
| *Leaves* | silk leaves |

### INSTRUCTIONS

*The flower.* Note that the pin-holes on this pricking are wider apart to take the thickness of the lamé thread. Work all petals in cloth stitch. Pin each finished petal onto the pillow, following the numbers on the pattern.

Petals 1, 2 & 3: start with 10 pairs wound in silver thread. Add 4 pairs in red, 2 at each pin-hole, as marked on the pricking.

Petal 4: start with 10 pairs wound in silver thread. Add 8 pairs wound in red, 2 at each pin-hole, as shown on the pattern.

### ASSEMBLY

*The flower.* Tie two red stamens to the pad at the top of a stem. Place between petals 1 & 3 and tie with a hitch knot. Then add petal No 2, the top petal, behind them. Finally add and tie petal No 4, the lip petal, in front. Tape the stem. Lightly curl the petals.

*The spray.* Make two flowers and combine with three slim long leaves cut from silk. The textures of the two materials will complement each other. Work as follows. Start by taping one of the three leaves to the top of a long main stem. Add the other two, staggered at ½ in (13 mm) intervals, each on a short stem. Add the two flowers, taping them one under the other. Turn the end of the taped stem into a loop to prevent damage if worn on clothing. This can be done round a pencil. A ribbon can be added to the spray if required. A pattern for a lamé ribbon is provided on p 68.

Prickings and layout for finished petals.

## DECORATIVE RIBBON

*Thread*    DMC 10 Fil d'Argent à broder. This is a lamé thread; use a colour of your own choice
*Stitch*    half-stitch, straight edges
*Symbols*    **x** starting point

## INSTRUCTIONS

Wind 10 pairs of bobbins and hang 2 pairs at each pin-hole marked **x**. Work in half-stitch throughout the pattern and tie off at the end. The length provided by the pricking will make the bow loops in one piece (see assembly diagram). Repeat half the length twice to make the tail pieces, and a quarter of the length for the knot.

## ASSEMBLY

*Bow loops.* Take the two ends under the centre of the ribbon and sew or bind them together with a thread. Make sure the cut threads are sandwiched between the two layers.

*Joining the bow to the tail pieces.* Place the bow over the cut ends of thread of the tail pieces. Hand sew together. Fold the tie piece over and under the join and sew together to make the knot.

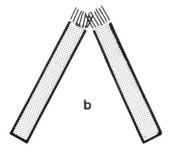

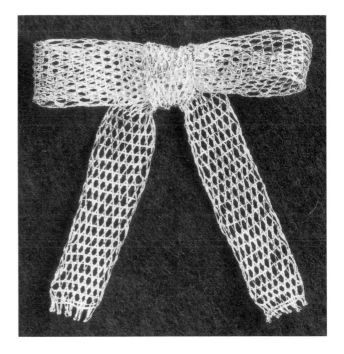

Assembly diagrams.

## LONG LACE LEAF

*Thread*    green Mettler 540 or 549
*Gimp*    green cotton-covered fine wire (millinery or rose wire)
*Stitch*    cloth stitch, straight edges
*Symbols*    **x** starting point

## INSTRUCTIONS

*The leaf.* 11 pairs of bobbins. Hang 11 pairs on the top pin. Work the first two pin-holes in cloth stitch; one at each edge. Divide the pairs as follows: 5 at each side with the weaver as an additional pair on one side. Lay the wire down the centre and work in cloth stitch across, making two twists on each side of the wire gimp.

On reaching the base, tie off as you would any leaf or petal. Use the gimp wire as the stem of the leaf, adding another if the gimp wire is not strong enough. Tape the stem.

This leaf can be used for the snowdrop, iris, daffodil or any long shaped leaf. The pattern can easily be made longer, if required.

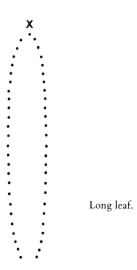

Long leaf.

# Botanical Notes
*by Janet M Darby*

### Forsythia
The shrub bears long erect sprigs of golden yellow, star shaped flowers closely clustered together. They are joined to the central stem by very short stalks. The flowers come out before the leaves.

### Snowdrop
Solitary white/green flowers with drooping heads. Where the flower stalk joins the main stem there is often a green leaf-like hood. The flower heads can be single or double.

The ridged grey-green slim leaves come from the bottom of the main flower stem.

### Crocus
Clumps of these vividly coloured flowers brighten our gardens in April. The mauve, purple, white, orange or yellow flowers come singly from an underground stem, called a corm.

If you look inside a crocus you will see that the flower consists of an inner and outer ring, each of 3 petals, with the inner petals overlapping the gaps between the outer ones. A yellow stamen lies inside each petal. The stigma, the part in the middle which collects the pollen, may also be brightly coloured and is sometimes fringed. The leaves are long and thin, bright green and often have a lighter stripe down the middle. They grow directly from the underground stem and form a ring round the flower.

### Winter jasmine
The long lax branches of this climbing shrub bear bright yellow star-like flowers that are scattered along the stems. The flowers have very short stalks and seem to come directly from the stems. They flower throughout the Winter months, giving a welcome splash of colour during the cold season.

### Primrose
The primrose is a native of Britain. Masses of pale yellow flowers are found in woods and on grassy banks in the Spring. Each flower is borne on a single stalk from a cluster of coarse mid-green leaves. One plant may bear up to a dozen flowers. The five notched petals have a dark yellow base which guides insects to the nectar and is often referred to as a 'honey guide'.

### Daffodil
Daffodils or narcissi are usually the first signs of spring. Flowers are borne singly. The six outer petals surround the trumpet, which can be large or small and can be frilled, and encloses yellow stamens. The petals may be white, orange or yellow and may be the same colour as the trumpet. The dark green lance-like leaves come from the bottom of the stem.

### Daisies
The common daisy is a very sophisticated plant. The daisy 'flower' is made up of many tiny flowers tightly packed together. The outer flowers form the petals; the inner flowers form the yellow centre and make the seeds. There are many varieties of daisies. The outer petals may be white, red, yellow, blue or orange. The centres may be black brown or yellow. The leaves may come from the flower stems or the base of the plant.

Japonica
Also called Ornamental Quince, or *Chaenomeles*. The cup-like flowers of this thorny bush grow in clusters almost directly on the woody stem. They lend themselves very well to flower arranging. The flowers range from orange to dark scarlet. The leaf of the Japonica, like its petals, is nearly round.

Narcissus
The old poet or pheasant eye narcissus was the model for this arrangement. This is an old and very popular garden plant. The white outer petals surround the small and characteristic orange trumpet.

Violet
One of the most loved of wild flowers. Single stalk flowers can be deep purple, mauve or white. The flower heads are made of five irregular petals. The heart-shaped leaves are light or mid green.

Iris
This is a very variable and very popular garden plant and comes in many colours and sizes. The flower has six petals, three upright and three bent back, forming a lip. There may be one or more flowers on each stem, but only one bud flowers at a time. The common bearded Iris ranges from white through pink, yellow, blue and mauve to dark purple and red. It gets its name from the rough patch on the lipped petal which is often brightly coloured. The grey-green sword-shaped leaves come from the bottom of the stem.

Garden cyclamen
This is one of the first of the Spring flowers. It bears small distinct flowers on short stalks in shades of pink, purple and white. The five petals, which are bent almost completely backwards, form a circular rim and reveal yellow stamens. The dark green heart-shaped leaves are marbled.

Wild pansy
The wild pansy is a native of Britain and flowers from April to November in grassy and bare places like sand dunes. The five petals are arranged with two above, two at the sides and one below. They may be yellow, violet or both. The petals may be veined giving the characteristic pansy 'face'. The flowers are born singly on short stalks attached to a main stem. The leaves grow from the main stem and are clustered around the base of the flower stems.

Forget-me-not
One of our favourite garden plants. The short stems bear two or three branches, each covered with clusters of up to ten small bright blue flowers with yellow centres. The young buds are at the top of the stem while the fully flowered ones are lower down. Small grey-green hairy leaves come directly from the stem.

Poppy
*Papaver orientale*, with its black blotches at the base of brilliant scarlet petals, yellow mottled seed pod and blue green stamens, was used as the poppy model. The hairy leaves are grey-green.

## Fuchsia

This double coloured flower grows in clusters. It has pendulous tube-shaped flowers, and petals in various colour combinations of pink, white, purple, red and (more rarely) orange. The outer sheaths of petals are turned back, revealing the inner petals and protruding stamens, and long club-shaped stigma. The leaves are oval and light green.

## Canary bird rose

Deep canary yellow flowers spring singly on arching sprays of this thorny bush. The scented flowers bloom in May/June. The mid green leaves are made up of six leaflets.

## Clematis montana

The striking white or pink flowers of this shrub can be seen in great profusion in our gardens in May, climbing up walls, along trellises and over trees. The dark green leaves are made up of three small leaflets.

## Lily

Often called the Day Lily because the buds flower for a day each, day after day. (It is also one of the flowers that stay open during the night!) The trumpet flowers grow on a stout stem and range from yellow through flame to deep mahogany. Their turned back petals are sometimes spotted and reveal a cluster of stamens which gives the flower its exotic appearance. The rush-like leaves are grass green.

## Freesia

This sweetly scented flower is nowadays grown mostly in greenhouses for the winter months. The flowers grow in single line sprays and open progressively from the bottom of the spray to the top. Colours range from white through pink, rose, purple and orange. The stamens are the same colour or slightly darker than the petals. The grass-like leaves come from the bottom of the stem.

## Orchid

There are many different kinds of orchid and some grow wild in Britain. However, the best known are the exotic and expensive greenhouse orchids which are bought for very special occasions. Their colours range from white, through pink, red, yellow and orange. The five outer petals surround an inner lipped cup. The cup may be spotted and often is a darker colour than the rest.

# Suppliers

A selection of suppliers who carry general or specialist materials required for making lace flowers. Many others may be found locally.

## Great Britain

Bedford Lace, 4a Newnham Street, Bedford MK40 3JR. Tel 0234 (Bedford) 47006.

Bucks Bobbins, Temple Lane Cottage, Littledean, Gloucester GL14 3NX. Tel 0594 (Dean) 22585.

Yvonne Dockree, Field Cottage, Rodsley, Brailford, Derbyshire DE6 3AL. Tel 033525 (Great Cubley) 469. *Stamens, and all materials for leaves.*

John & Jennifer Ford, 5 Squirrels Hollow, Boney Hay, Walsall, Staffordshire WS7 8YS. Tel 05436 (Walsall) 74598.

Maureen Foster, 17 Bullbridge Road, Wilton, Salisbury, Wiltshire SP2 0LE. *Preserving crystals for natural leaves.*

Denis Hornsby, 159 High Street, Burton Latimer, Northants NN15 5RL. Tel 053672 (Burton Latimer) 2791.

Lacecraft Supplies, 8 Hill View, Sherington, Bucks MK16 9NJ. Tel 0908 (Milton Keynes) 610624.

Larkfield Crafts, 4 Island Cottages, Mapledurwell, Basingstoke, Hampshire RG25 2LU. Tel 0265 (Basingstoke) 476585. *Stamens, and a very fine ribbon.*

Dorothy Pearce, 5 Fulshaw Ave, Wilmslow, Cheshire SK9 5JA. Tel 0652 (Wilmslow) 522176.

Sebalace, 76 Main Street, Addingham, Ilkley, West Yorks LS29 0PL. Tel 0943 (Ilkley) 831201.

Arthur Sells, Lane Cove, 49 Pedley Lane, Clifton, Shefford, Beds. Tel 0462 (Hitchin) 814725.

Southgate Handicrafts, 63 Southgate Street, Gloucester GL1 1TX. Tel 0452 (Gloucester) 20662.

## USA

Beggar's Lace, 3036 E 6th Ave, Denver, CO 80206. *All kinds of threads including silk threads.*

Frivolité, 15526 Densmore N, Seattle, WA 98133. Tel (206) 364-9646.

Robin & Russ Handweavers, 533 North Adams Street, McMinnville, Oregon 97128. Tel (503) 472-5760.

Van Sciver Bobbin Lace, 130 Cascadilla Park, Ithaca, NY 14850. Tel (607) 277- 0498.

## Other Lace, Costume and Embroidery Books

**The Needlework of Mary Queen of Scots** Margaret Swain
0 903585 22 7    280 × 212mm, 128p, 89pl incl 12 colour, paperback

**Bedfordshire Lace Patterns** – A selection by Margaret Turner
0 903585 21 9    280 × 210mm, 112p, 145ill, folding sheet, limpbound

**Manual of Bedfordshire Lace** Pamela Robinson
0 903585 20 0    247 × 233mm, 112p, 151ill, limpbound

**Lace Flowers and How to Make Them** Joyce Willmot
0 903585 23 5    187 × 156mm, 76p, 46pl & diagr incl colour, hardbound

**The Technique & Design of Cluny Lace** L Paulis/Maria Rutgers
0 903585 18 9    220 × 174mm, 96p, 130ill, hardbound

**Victorian Costume & Costume Accessories** Anne Buck
0 903585 17 0    220 × 174mm, 224p, 90ill, paperback

**Le Pompe 1559** Santina Levey/Pat Payne
(Patterns for Venetian Bobbin Lace)
0 903585 16 2    243 × 177mm, 128p, 97ill, paperback

**Teach Yourself Torchon Lace** Eunice Arnold
0 903585 08 1    240 × 190mm, 40p, 6workcards, 27ill, limpbound

**Pillow Lace – A Practical Hand-book** E Mincoff/M Marriage
0 903585 10 3    216 × 138mm, 304p, 2worksheets, 90ill, hardbound

**Victorian Lace** Patricia Wardle
0 903585 13 8    222 × 141mm, 304p, 82pl, hardbound

**Thomas Lester His Lace & E Midlands Industry 1820–1905** Anne Buck
0 903585 09 X    280 × 210mm, 120p, 55pl, hardbound

**The Romance of the Lace Pillow** Thomas Wright
0 903585 12 X    222 × 141mm, 340p, 50pl, hardbound

**Tailor's Pattern Book 1589** Juan de Alcega
(Libro de Geometria, Pratica y Traça)
0 903585 06 5    279 × 203mm, 244p, 137ill, clothbound

### In preparation

**Embroidery in 18th Century Britain** Patricia Wardle
0 903585 19 7    280 × 212mm,
c.350p, 150ill incl col pl, limpbound

### Books on Textiles from:

RUTH BEAN Publishers
VICTORIA FARMHOUSE
CARLTON
BEDFORD MK43 7LP
ENGLAND